From Your Friends At **The MAILBOX®**

W9-AHQ-436

NOVEMBER

A MONTH OF REPRODUCIBLES AT YOUR FINGERTIPS!

Kindergarten

Project Editor:
Angie Kutzer

Contributing Editors:
Ada Goren, Allison E. Ward

Writers:
Joe Appleton, Susan Bunyan, Susan DeRiso,
Rhonda Dominguez, Henry Fergus, Diane Gilliam,
Lucia Kemp Henry, Kathleen Padilla, Kelli Plaxco

Art Coordinator:
Clevell Harris

Artists:
Pam Crane, Teresa Davidson, Clevell Harris,
Lucia Kemp Henry, Susan Hodnett,
Kimberly Richard, Rebecca Saunders,
Donna K. Teal, Jennifer L. Tipton

Cover Artist:
Jennifer L. Tipton

www.themailbox.com

©1999 by THE EDUCATION CENTER, INC.
All rights reserved.
ISBN10 #1-56234-281-9 • ISBN13 #978-156234-281-4

Manufactured in the United States
10 9 8 7 6 5 4

Table Of Contents

To Do:

Special Dates:

Books To Check Out:

MEETINGS:

MATERIALS TO COLLECT:

November
Classroom Themes:

Duties This Month:

Birthdays:

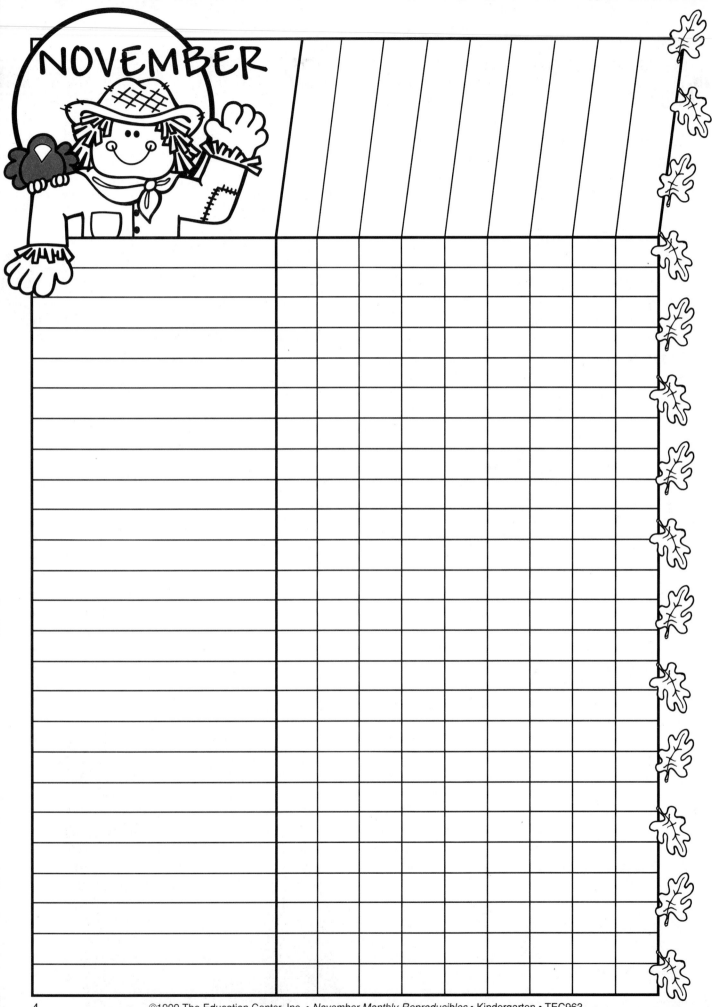

NOVEMBER

©1999 The Education Center, Inc. • *November Monthly Reproducibles* • Kindergarten • TEC963

Once your youngsters are introduced to the alphabet, use these activities to help them get to know their letters better.

Sing-Along Scarecrow

This cute scarecrow loves to sing the alphabet song! Duplicate page 7 onto tagboard for each child. Use an X-acto® knife to slit the scarecrow's mouth along the two dotted lines. Have the child color her scarecrow, cut it out, and attach a large craft stick to the back to make a handle. Direct her to cut out the letter strip; then help her thread it through the scarecrow's mouth as shown. Tape the ends of the strip together to make a loop. Now it's time to sing! Encourage the child to pull the strip to show each letter as she sings its name in the song.

Patchwork Pairs

Have youngsters use their visual-discrimination skills to find matching letters on the scarecrow's patches. Give each child a copy of page 8. Have him find each letter pair, draw a matching design on the blank letter, and then color the pair identically.

A Scarecrow Surprise

Distinguishing between letters, numerals, and shapes isn't so scary in this activity. Give each child a copy of page 9. Read the color key aloud and have students color the crayons the appropriate colors to set up the code. Then encourage each child to work independently to reveal the scarecrow hiding in the puzzle. Surprise!

Crows In The Corn

This alphabet display will give your little ones something to crow about! To prepare, obtain a supply of dried corn kernels (or use popcorn kernels) and duplicate page 10 onto tagboard for each child. Instruct the child to color and cut out her pattern. Then have her write on the pattern the first initial of her name, the letter of the week, her favorite letter, or any other letter choice that you determine. (You may want to label each child's pattern in advance to emphasize correct formation and size.) To complete the project, the child glues on corn kernels to trace her letter. After the glue is dry, display students' finished projects on a bulletin board titled "A Bumper Crop Of Letters."

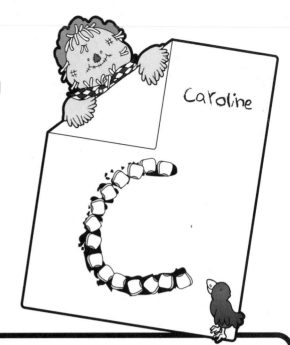

Letter-Go-Round

This smart scarecrow has come straight out of the cornfield to help your youngsters learn to match uppercase and lowercase letters. Duplicate page 11 onto construction paper for each child. Instruct the child to color the scarecrow and its arms. Then have the child cut out the wheel and arm pieces. Help her use a brad to attach the arms to the center of the wheel where indicated. Encourage students to use their wheels for independent practice or, for a whole-group activity, call out the name of a letter and have each child make her scarecrow point to the corresponding letters on her wheel.

Show What You Know

Add some straw-filled fun to your assessment of students' letter-recognition skills with this reproducible. Make one copy of page 12 and program the scarecrow's patches with letters that you have studied thus far in the school year. Duplicate this page for each child. Ask each child to tell you the name of each letter on his sheet. Instruct him to color the patches of the letters that were named correctly. Then invite him to color the rest of the picture. Save this page in each child's portfolio to show parents during fall conferences.

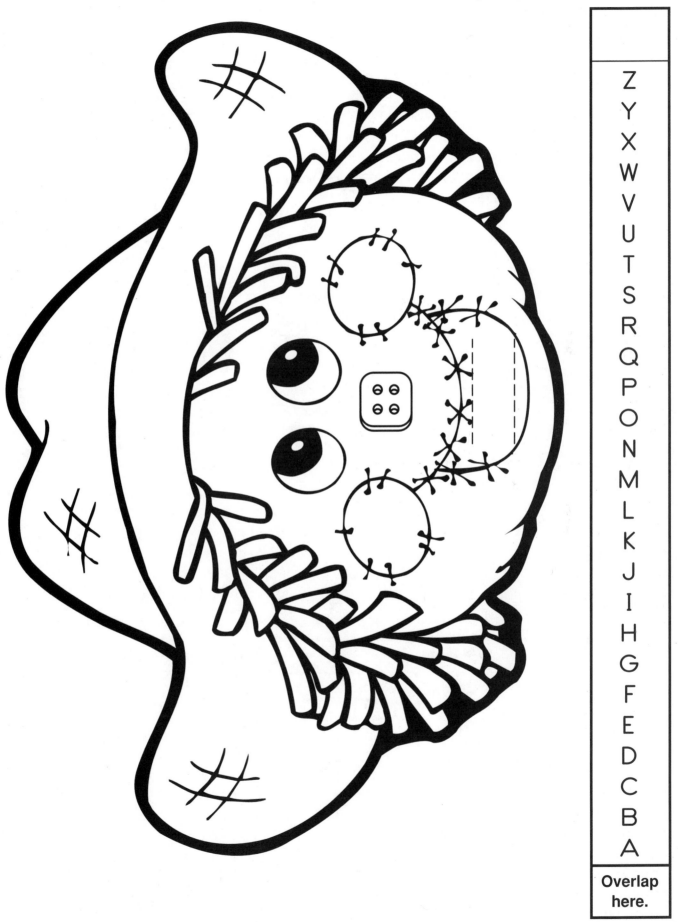

Z Y X W V U T S R Q P O N M L K J I H G F E D C B A

Overlap here.

Name _____

Patchwork Pairs

Find each letter pair.
Draw the matching pattern.
Color the patches the same.

©1999 The Education Center, Inc. • *November Monthly Reproducibles* • Kindergarten • TEC963

A Scarecrow Surprise

Color by the code.

letters—green   numerals—blue   shapes—yellow

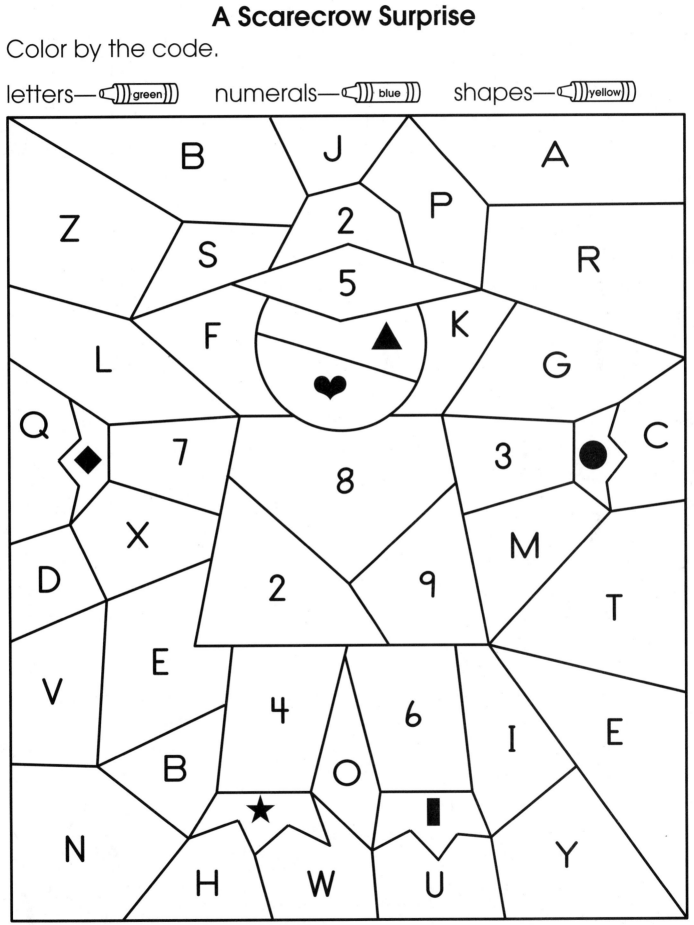

Pattern

Use with "Crows In The Corn" on page 6.

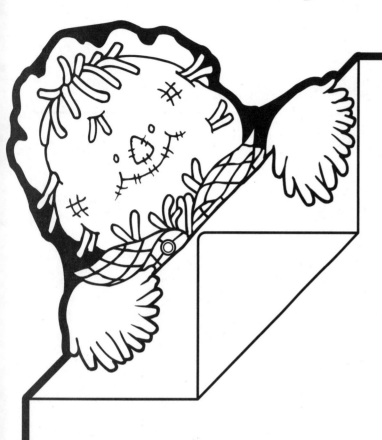

Name _____

Show What You Know

Say each letter's name.
Color the letter patches that you identified correctly.

©1999 The Education Center, Inc. • *November Monthly Reproducibles* • Kindergarten • TEC963

Perfectly Peanut Butter!

On crackers, sandwiches, and cookies, too—we love peanut butter, how 'bout you? Spread this favorite snack across your curriculum during Peanut Butter Lovers' Month in November.

A Smooth And Creamy Transition

During Peanut Butter Lovers' Month, try this twist to line up your youngsters or to choose volunteers. Cut out a class supply of construction-paper peanut shapes. Write a different child's name on each peanut; then attach a large paper clip to each one. Place the peanut cutouts in a cleaned plastic peanut butter jar. Attach a strip of magnetic tape to one side of a plastic knife (or another dull butter knife). To choose a participant, simply stick the knife in the jar and pull out a peanut!

We Go Together...

Like peanut butter and jelly! Entice youngsters to think of associations in this activity. With your students, brainstorm objects that depend on or complement one another, such as salt and pepper or a hammer and nail. Discuss the association between each pair of objects. Then give each child a copy of page 14 to match items that are commonly referred to as dynamic duos.

Popular Peanut Butter Book Picks

My First Book Of How Things Are Made: Crayons, Jeans, Guitars, Peanut Butter, And More
Written by George Jones
Published by Cartwheel Books

Peanut Butter And Jelly: A Play Rhyme
Illustrated by Nadine Bernard Westcott
Published by E. P. Dutton

Reese's Pieces® Peanut Butter: Counting Board Book
Written by Jerry Pallotta
Published by Corporate Board Books, Inc.

Name _____

We Go Together Like...

 Color.

Cut.

Glue.

©1999 The Education Center, Inc. • *November Monthly Reproducibles* • Kindergarten • TEC963

Bonus Box: Think of another example of associated items and draw them on the back of your paper.

SERVE UP SOME Sandwiches

November 3 has been designated as Sandwich Day, a day to recognize the "inventor" of the fastest, easiest way to eat a meal. John Montague, Fourth Earl of Sandwich, was born on this day in 1718. Celebrate these two-fisted treats with this double-decker load of learning.

Please Pass The Sandwich

What do you like in a sandwich? Everyone contributes an ingredient in this memory game. With your youngsters seated in a circle, have the first player begin the game by saying, "Today I made a sandwich. I put [peanut butter] on it." The first player pantomimes passing a sandwich to the next player. The next player repeats the original sentences and adds an ingredient: "Today I made a sandwich. I put [peanut butter and bananas] on it." Play continues with each player repeating what has previously been said and then adding another ingredient. Once the list gets too challenging for your group, start the sandwich-making again.

For added fun, cut out two bread slices and a class supply of colorful "ingredient" circles from craft foam. Give each child a circle; then give the bread to the first player. As each child adds his ingredient, students can actually see how large the sandwich is becoming. Now *that's* a sandwich that's hard to forget!

Pile On The Shapes

Reinforce shape recognition and provide some fine-motor practice as your little ones construct these shape sandwiches. Duplicate pages 17 and 18 onto white construction paper. Have each child prepare her ingredients as described below. After the paint dries, direct her to cut out the pieces, assemble them into a sandwich, and staple them together on one side.

Bread Squares: Color brown around the edges to make crusts. Write your name on the cover. Color the letters on the back cover.

Cheese Triangle: Color yellow; then make holes with a hole puncher to resemble Swiss cheese.

Meat Rectangle: Sponge-paint (or use cotton balls) with a mixture of red and brown paint.

Tomato Circle: Fingerpaint with red paint.

Pickle Oval: Cover with green fingerprints.

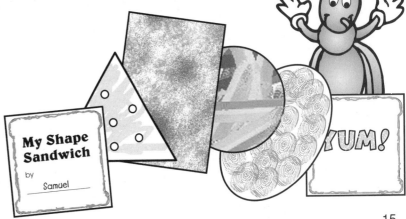

My Shape Sandwich
by Samuel

Sandwich Steps

Use the reproducible on page 16 to work on students' sequencing skills. Have each child color the pictures on a copy of the page and cut them out. Then direct her to sequence the steps and glue the ordered pictures to a strip of construction paper. Provide peanut butter, jelly, bread, plastic knives, and paper plates, for youngsters to make real-life applications of their successful sequences.

Name _____

Sandwich Steps

 Color. ✂ Cut. Glue.

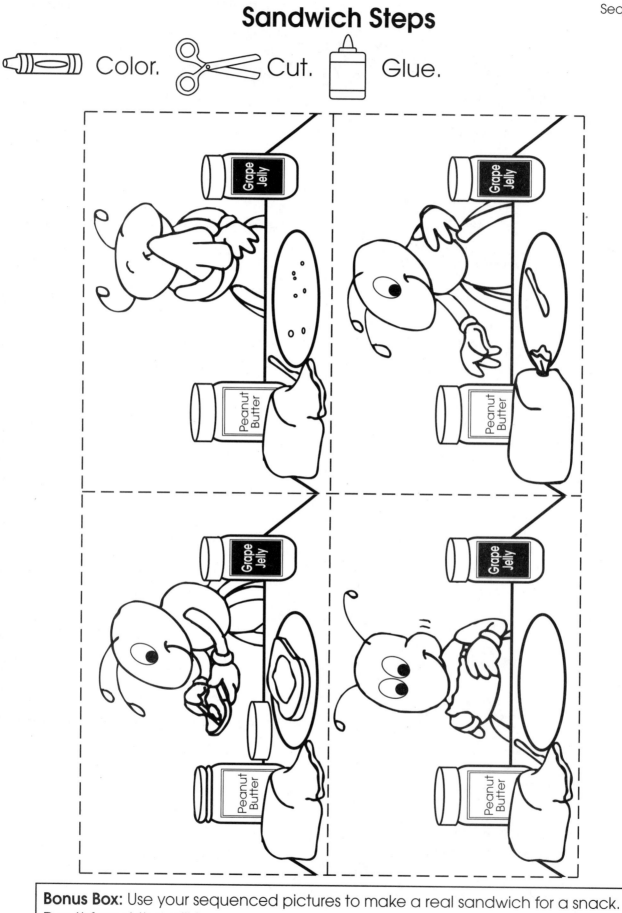

Bonus Box: Use your sequenced pictures to make a real sandwich for a snack. Don't forget the milk!

bread

My Shape Sandwich

by

_____

meat

YUM!

Patterns

Use with "Pile On The Shapes" on page 15.

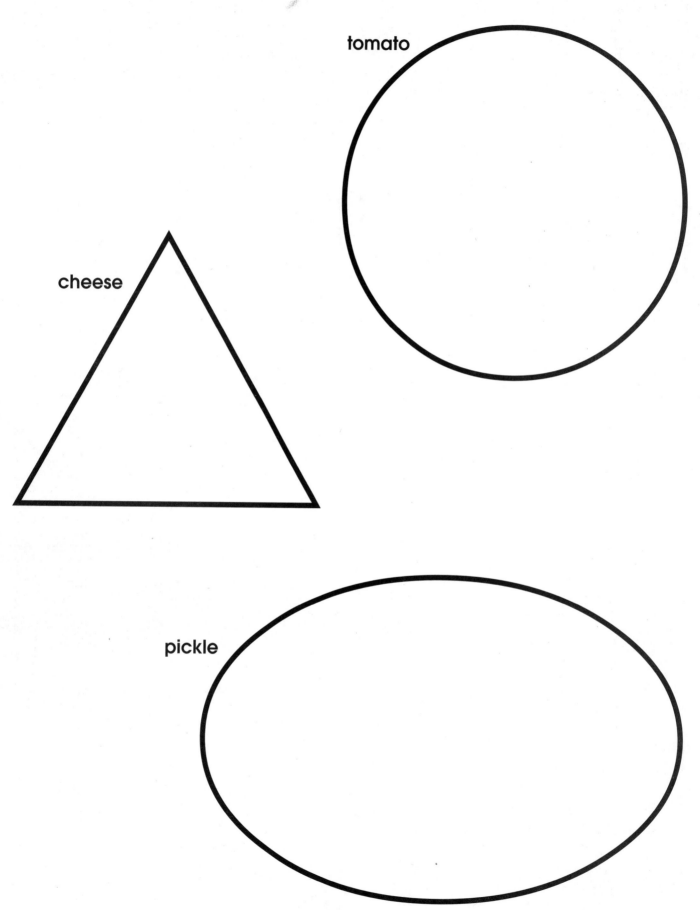

tomato

cheese

pickle

Signs Of Safety

Move learning out of the classroom and into the environment with these activities that integrate some basic-skills reinforcement with signs that keep us safe.

The Many Sides Of Signs

Introduce the many different shapes of signs by doing this counting activity. Duplicate page 20 for each child. Have him look at each sign, count its sides, and record the number in the blank provided. Extend the activity by asking volunteers to tell the shape and meaning of each sign.

A Green Light For Safety

Reinforce safe scenarios with the reproducible on page 22. Give each child a copy of the page. Direct him to look at each picture and decide whether or not it's showing a safe thing to do. If the picture depicts a safe action, the child colors the green light on the corresponding stoplight. If it is an unsafe action, the child colors the red light. Get ready—this activity will give the green light to lots of safety discussions!

Searching For Signs

This visual-discrimination puzzle will have youngsters on the lookout for signs. Give each child a copy of page 21. Discuss the signs displayed along the bottom of the page; then send each child searching for the same signs in the busy city scene. Once the signs are found and circled, have the student color the scene.

Signs To Read

Reading and discussing the meaning of signs is a perfect emergent reading activity to incorporate environmental print. Make a poster of various signs around your neighborhood. (Consider taking instant photos of actual signs or enlarging and cutting out signs from a driver's education manual.) Duplicate page 23 for each child. Have him use the poster to label each of the signs on his page. Once students have their pages completed, discuss the meaning of each sign and where you might find it. Then, as a follow-up, have each child complete a copy of page 24, gluing each sign to its corresponding scene.

Name _____

The Many Sides Of Signs

How many sides?

Count.

Write.

©1999 The Education Center, Inc. • *November Monthly Reproducibles* • Kindergarten • TEC963

Searching For Signs

Find and circle these signs in the picture above:

Name _____

A Green Light For Safety

Look at each picture.

Is it safe?

Color the stoplight. green —yes   red —no

Name _____

Signs To Read

Use the poster to label each sign.
Practice reading the signs.

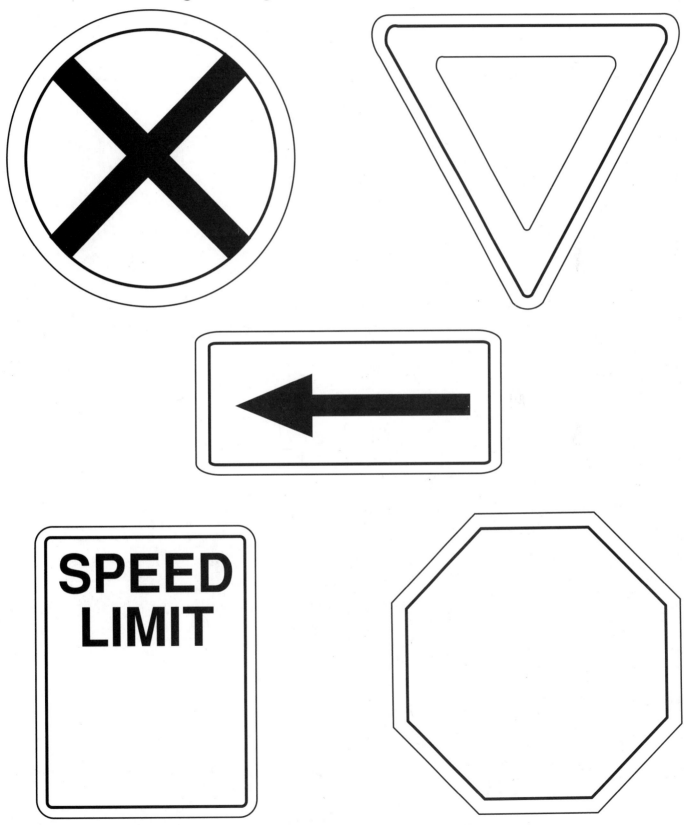

Name _____

Show Me A Sign!

Cut.

Glue.

24

Here are some "purr-fect" ways to incorporate those fun, furry felines into your curriculum. So lick your paws and get ready to pounce!

Kitty Cat Cookies

This snack idea is the cat's meow! Gather a class supply of the items listed on page 26. Duplicate page 26 for each child. Have her color the pictures, then cut the paper along the dotted lines. Direct her to glue the strips in sequential order onto a piece of construction paper. Now encourage the child to use the recipe to make her own kitty cat cookie.

Alphabet "A-mews-ment"

Yarn here, yarn there—look at the yarn everywhere! Encourage your little kittens to search through the yarn heaps on page 27 to uncover the hidden letters. Give each child a copy of the page and have him color each letter a different color. For added fun, invite him to glue yarn around the outlines of the letters.

Is Th*at* A C*at*?

Promote phonemic awareness with this activity that reinforces the *-at* rime. Make a transparency from page 29. With the transparency on your overhead projector, read one of the words to your class. Ask a student volunteer to tell you if the word has the same ending as the word *cat.* If it does, have him come up and draw ears, eyes, a nose, and whiskers to turn the word into a cat. If the word doesn't have the *-at* ending, have him draw squiggles over it, designating it as a yarn ball. Continue drawing cats or yarn balls for the remaining words on the sheet.

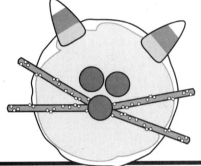

Curl Up With These Books!

Use the literature list contained on these bookmarks (page 30) to add a little fur and frolic to your storytimes. Then duplicate a class supply of the bookmarks. Have each child color one, cut it out, and take it home to encourage more "purr-fect" reading with parents.

Take A Peek

Use the pattern on page 28 to frame students' cat-related writing or artwork. Provide each child with a construction-paper copy of the pattern. Have her color the pattern and cut it out; then attach her work to the cat's paws. Display the cats together with the title "Paws For Applause!"

25

Kitty Cat Cookie

You will need:

 1 cookie

1 paper plate

3 M&M's® candies

1 plastic knife

2 candy corn pieces

yellow tinted icing (or another cat fur color)

4 pretzel sticks

1 Spread icing on the cookie.

2 Make the eyes and nose.

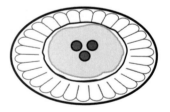

3 Add ears and whiskers. Meow!

Alphabet "A-mews-ment"

Find the hidden letters.

Color each letter a different color.

Cat Pattern
Use with "Take A Peek" on page 25.

Is Th*at* A C*at*?

Listen closely for the –*at*.
If you hear it, draw a cat.

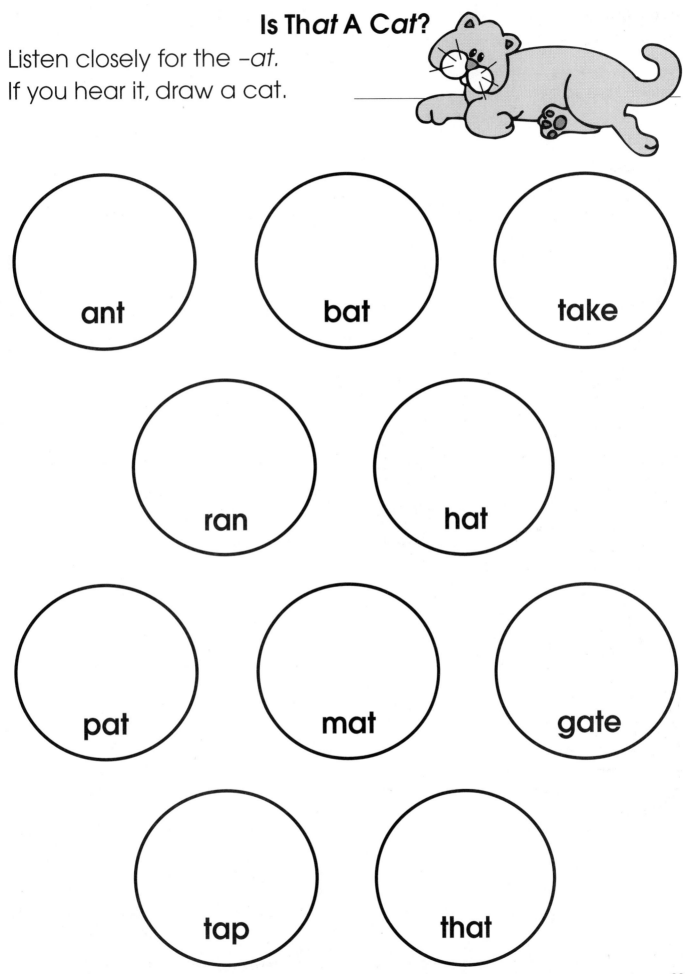

ant

bat

take

ran

hat

pat

mat

gate

tap

that

Here are some "purr-fect" picks for our reading time together.

Michael And The Cats
Written by Barbara Abercrombie

Have You Seen My Cat?
Written by Eric Carle

The Cat Who Lost His Purr
Written by Michele Coxon

Feathers For Lunch
Written by Lois Ehlert

Mama Cat Has Three Kittens
Written by Denise Fleming

Wee G.
Written by Harriet M. Ziefert

Kitten For A Day
Written by Ezra Jack Keats

When Cats Dream
Written by Dav Pilkey

Ginger
Written by Charlotte Voake

Can we curl up with one of these books tonight? Meow!

©1999 The Education Center, Inc.

Here are some "purr-fect" picks for our reading time together.

Michael And The Cats
Written by Barbara Abercrombie

Have You Seen My Cat?
Written by Eric Carle

The Cat Who Lost His Purr
Written by Michele Coxon

Feathers For Lunch
Written by Lois Ehlert

Mama Cat Has Three Kittens
Written by Denise Fleming

Wee G.
Written by Harriet M. Ziefert

Kitten For A Day
Written by Ezra Jack Keats

When Cats Dream
Written by Dav Pilkey

Ginger
Written by Charlotte Voake

Can we curl up with one of these books tonight? Meow!

©1999 The Education Center, Inc.

Space Is The Place!

A *real* trip to outer space may be out of the question, but that doesn't mean your little ones can't use their imaginations. After all, childhood dreams of space travel will create the astronauts of the future!

Shuttle Mission Booklet

Your youngsters' feet may be firmly planted on Earth, but they can head into outer space on a space shuttle mission with this reproducible booklet. To prepare, duplicate a class supply of pages 32–38 onto white construction paper. Read through the directions below and gather the necessary materials. Have each child cut out her cover, pages, and patterns. Invite her to complete her booklet following these steps:

Cover: Color the Moon yellow and the area around the shuttle black. Draw stars with glitter glue. Write your name on the line.

Page 1: Glue the three text boxes to the page. Draw a picture of yourself as an astronaut in the space to the right.

Page 2: Draw a face and hair for the astronaut. Color the face shield on the helmet pattern black; then glue it to the page.

Page 3: Glue the shuttle pattern to the page. Color the Earth picture and draw stars and planets on the page.

Page 4: Cut out the circle on the helmet. Tape your school photo behind the page so your face shows in the opening. Color the Moon pattern yellow; then glue it to the page.

Page 5: Color the trees pattern; then glue it to the page. Color the rest of the picture.

Help each child stack her completed cover and pages in order; then staple the booklet along the left side. Mission accomplished!

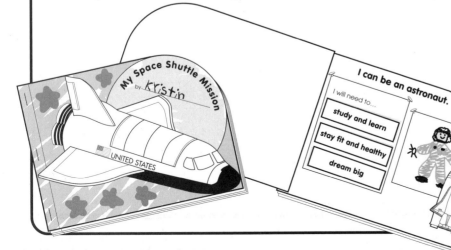

Astronaut Imaginings

What will space travel be like when your students grow up? Encourage them to show you what they imagine the future holds with this out-of-this-world display. Read the following poem to your students; then ask them to each draw a picture of a futuristic spacecraft. Display the drawings, along with a copy of the poem, on a bulletin board covered in black paper.

An astronaut travels
to a distant place.
He flies in a shuttle
into outer space.
Would you like to
travel to space far
away?
A spacecraft like this
might take *you*
there one day!

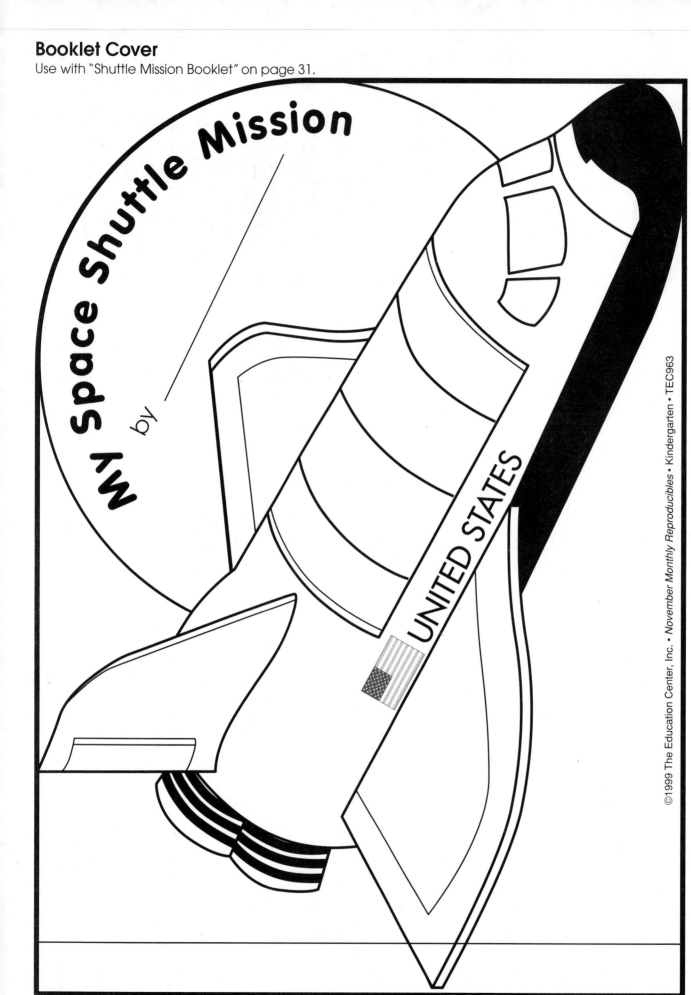

My Space Shuttle Mission

by

UNITED STATES

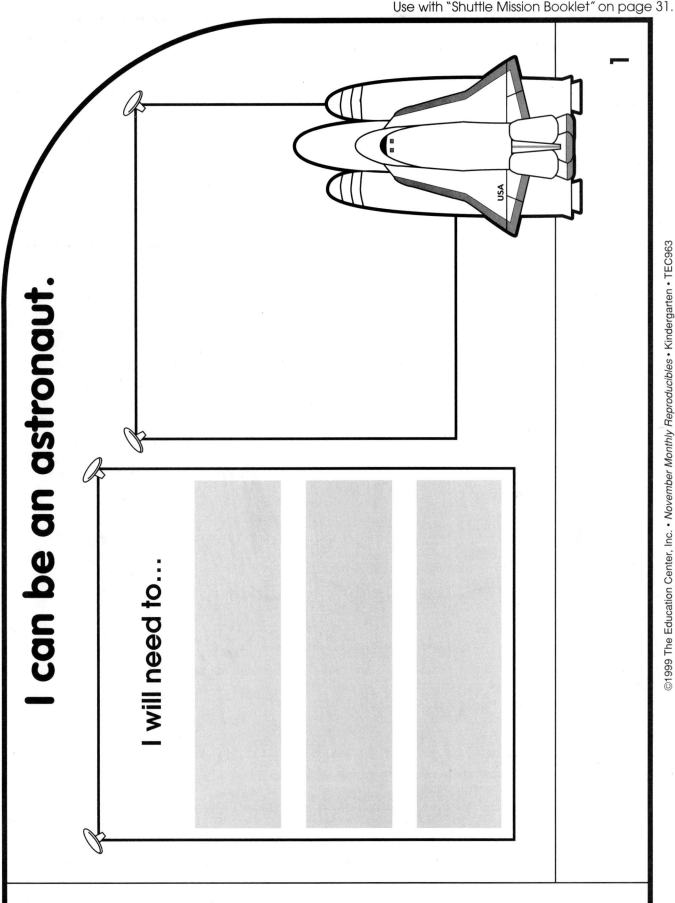

1

I can be an astronaut.

I will need to...

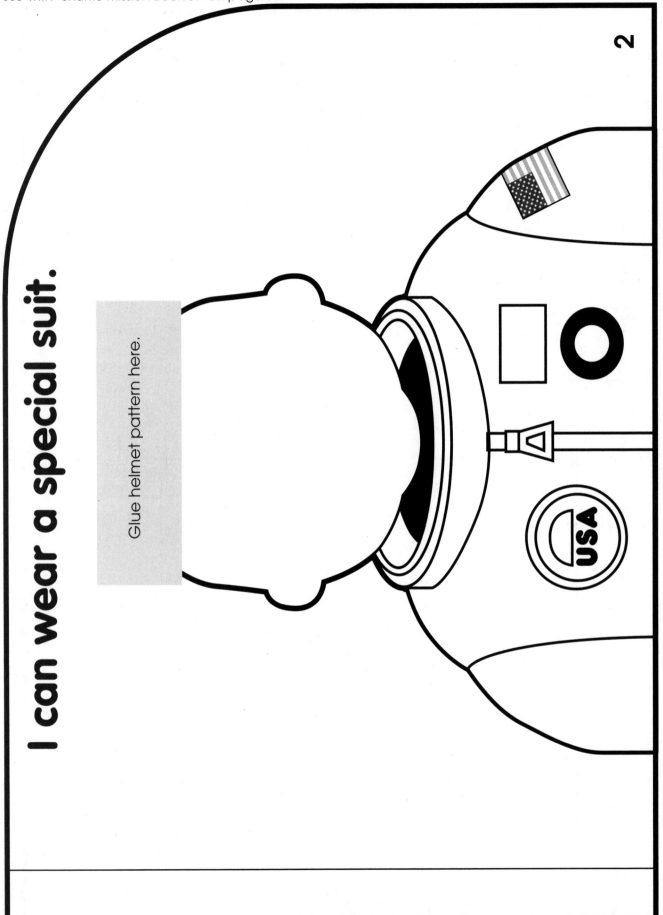

I can wear a special suit.

Glue helmet pattern here.

2

3

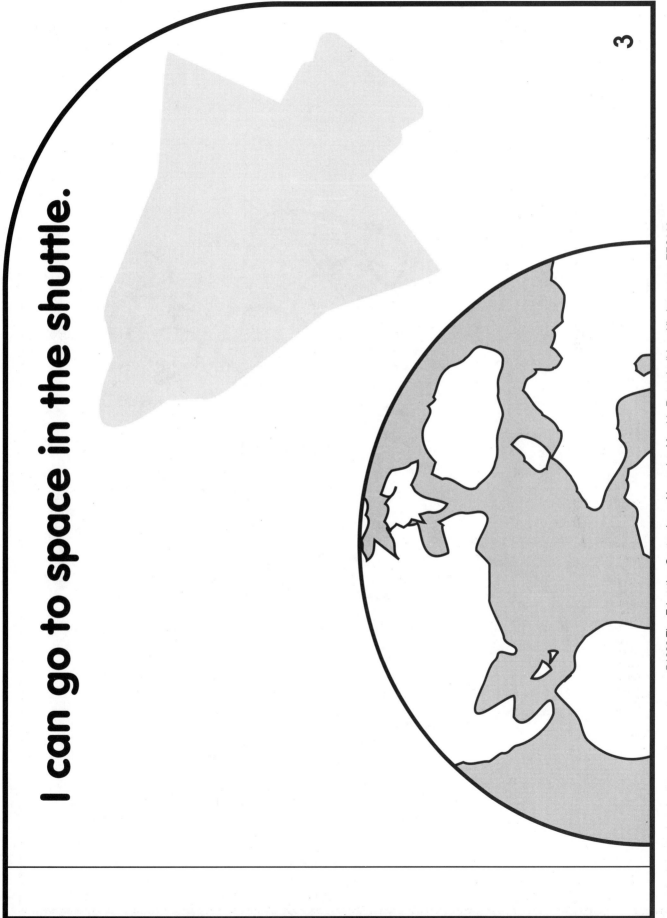

I can go to space in the shuttle.

4

I can take a space walk!

Cut this out.

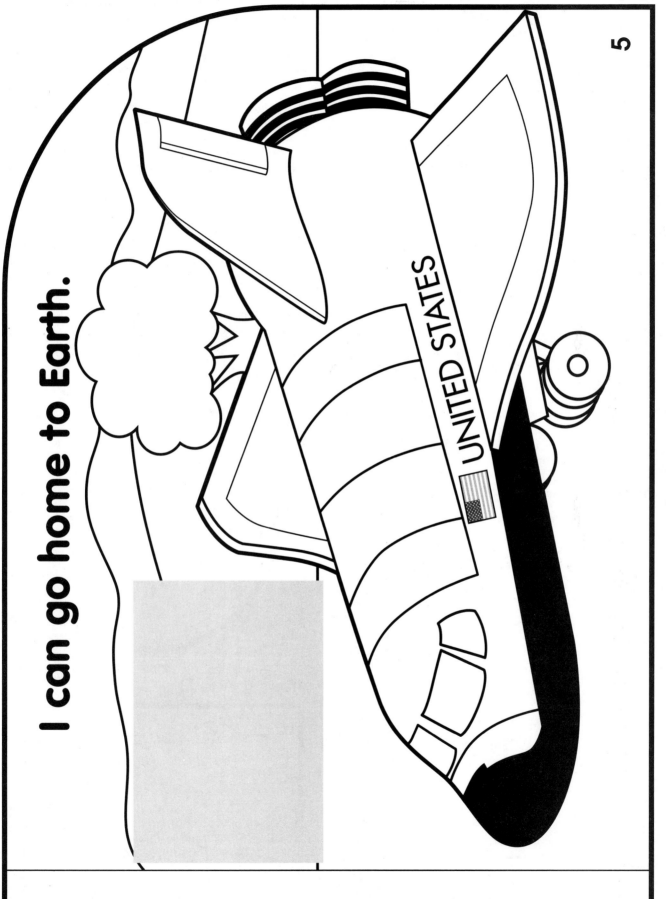

I can go home to Earth.

5

UNITED STATES

Booklet Patterns

Use with "Shuttle Mission Booklet" on page 31.

shuttle (page 3)

text boxes (page 1)

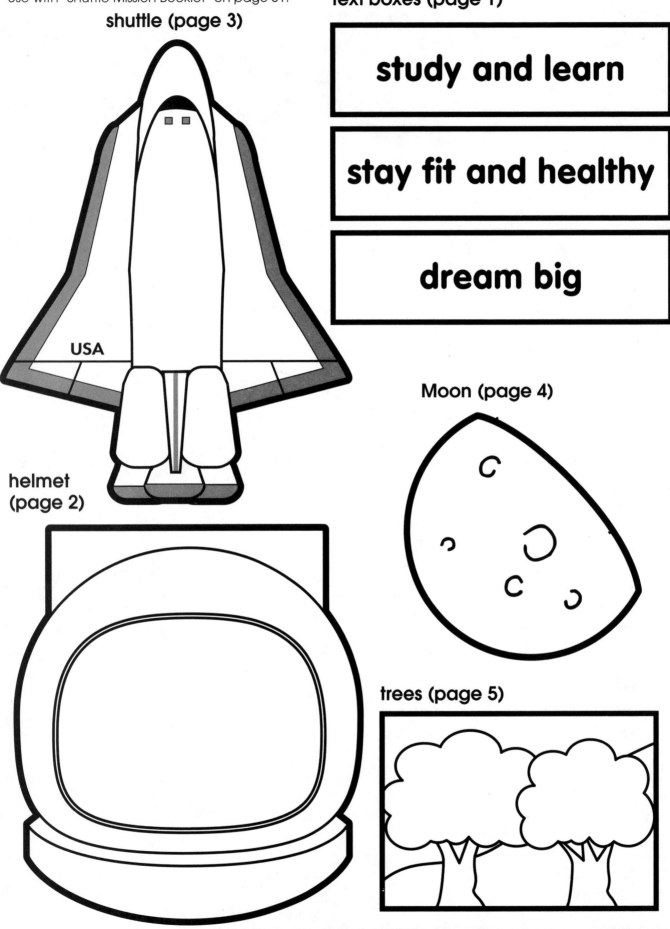

study and learn

stay fit and healthy

dream big

USA

Moon (page 4)

helmet (page 2)

trees (page 5)

Let's Read!

Use this timesaving collection of reproducibles to celebrate National Children's Book Week, the third week in November. Then watch as your little ones' love for reading lives happily ever after.

Advertise The Event

Have your youngsters make these personalized posters to advertise National Children's Book Week. Duplicate the poster on page 41 for each child; then cut it out along the bold lines. Also cut out the circle as indicated on each copy. Finish preparations by cutting a class supply of 3 1/2" x 4 1/2" construction-paper cards.

To make a poster, have each child color her page and write her name where indicated. Next help her tape a photo of herself to the back of her page so that her face shows through the opening. Instruct the child to draw her favorite book character in the box. Fill in the three dictated clues about her character. Staple one side of the card to the top of the illustration box to cover the character, as shown. Mount the posters on separate colorful sheets of construction paper and display them around school. Your librarian will thank you!

Celebrate Children's Book Week with *Samantha*

My favorite character:
1. is big
2. is red
3. barks

Can you guess who it is?

READ MORE ABOUT IT!

Clifford!

Read To Me

National Children's Book Week is a great time to encourage parents to read with their youngsters. Send home construction-paper copies of page 42. Instruct each parent to have his child color in a segment of the bookworm to record each night they read together. When the worm is completely colored, direct the parent to cut it out and return it to school. Then laminate the worms and add wiggle eyes to make a bookmark keepsake for each child.

Thank An Author

Your students are sure to have all-time favorite books—ones that really got them hooked on reading. So why not thank the authors with these pop-up cards? Give each child a copy of page 43. Have the child color and cut out the card pattern. Help him to crease the pattern forward and backward on the dotted lines. Then help him fold his pattern horizontally and vertically on the dotted lines to make a card. To make the heart pop out, fold it forward and downward on the dotted lines at the bottom of the heart. Have the student write the author's name on the front of the card where indicated. Then direct him to sign his name inside the card. If desired, have each child draw his favorite character inside the heart or decorate the heart with glitter and sequins.

Check the American Library Association's Web site for help in finding authors' addresses. The Web address www.ala.org/parentspage/greatsites will provide links to several favorite authors' home pages. Happy National Children's Book Week!

Goin' On A Book Hunt

Celebrate the variety of book formats with this fun scavenger hunt. Have children search your classroom or arrange with the librarian ahead of time to complete the search in the media center. Give each child a copy of the list on page 44. Read the list aloud and discuss the types of books to be found so that each child is familiar with the picture cues. Then let the search begin! On your signal, have children search on their own or in pairs to find as many books listed as possible. After an adequate amount of time, call students together and see if anyone found every book listed. Reward your search party with *what?* A good story, of course!

Celebrate
Children's Book Week
with _____

(name)

My favorite character:

1. _____

2. _____

3. _____

Can you guess who it is?

Cut this out.

Staple card here.

READ MORE ABOUT IT!

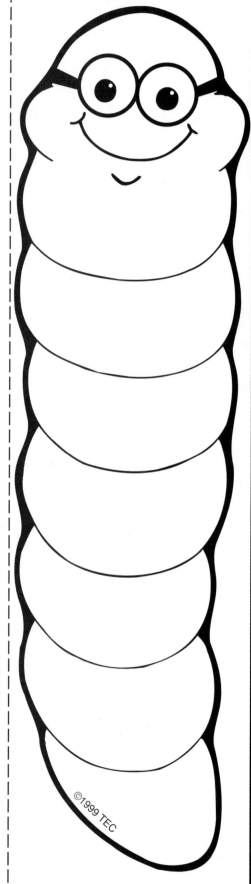

Dear Parent,

    We will be celebrating National Children's Book Week on November _____. Please help us continue the celebration by setting aside a few minutes each night to read with your child. After each night's reading, have your child color in one segment of the bookworm on the side of this page. When the worm is completed, cut it out and return it to school. The worm will be used to make a special keepsake for your child.

    Hopefully, you've seen the benefits of reading with your child, not to mention the fun you have together! Thanks for participating. Now here's a special award for you to cut out and wear with pride. Congratulations!

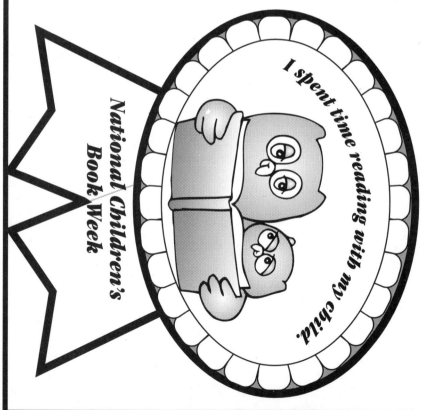

National Children's Book Week

I spent time reading with my child.

©1999 TEC

©1999 The Education Center, Inc.

Dear_____,

you got me hooked...

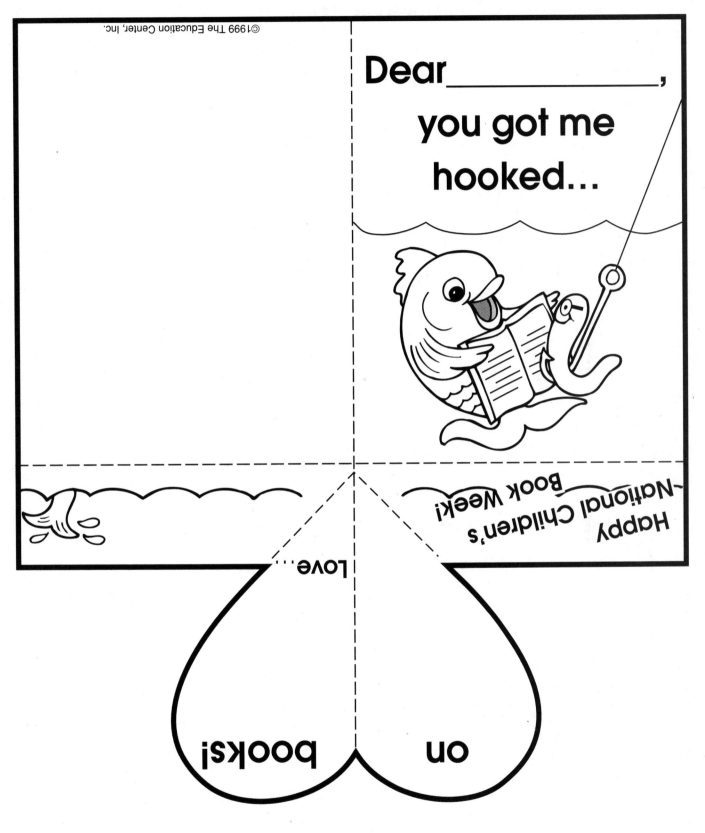

Happy
National Children's
Book Week!

Love...

books! on

Goin' On A Book Hunt

Find an example of each book.
Color each bookworm after you find the book.

1. a book with no words

2. an alphabet book

3. a really small book

4. a really big book

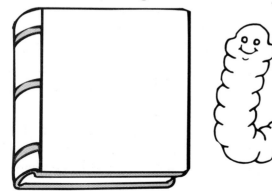

5. a book with more than 10 pages

6. a board book

7. a book about animals

8. a book about food

Let's Give Thanks!

Each year Americans celebrate Thanksgiving on the last Thursday in November. Here's a feast of activities your little ones will be thankful for!

The First Thanksgiving

Introduce youngsters to the first Thanksgiving with this sequencing activity. Read aloud or paraphrase a book describing the first Thanksgiving; then discuss the events with your students. Give each child a copy of page 47. Have her color, cut apart, and sequence the pictures. Then instruct her to glue the ordered pictures in place. There you have it—the first Thanksgiving in pictures!

Turkey Feather Match

This feathery file-folder game is stuffed with math skills. To prepare, duplicate pages 48 and 49 onto tagboard. Color the turkey and feather cards; then cut them apart. To create pockets, glue each turkey card along its sides and bottom inside a file folder. Cut out the game label and directions. Glue the label to the file tab and the game directions inside the folder, as shown. Tape the sides and bottom of a resealable sandwich bag to the back of the folder. Store the feather cards inside the bag.

To use this game, a child tucks each feather card into the corresponding turkey pocket. For added fun, use colorful craft feathers instead of cards, and have the child put the correct number of feathers in each pocket.

An "A-maize-ing" Gift

Get your youngsters in the Thanksgiving spirit by making these festive decorations that resemble Indian corn. To prepare, duplicate a class supply of page 50. Pour small amounts of red, yellow, orange, and white tempera paint into separate shallow containers. Place a supply of cotton swabs near the paints. Then read the poem on the corn pattern to your students.

To make one ornament, cut out the husk and corn patterns. Color both sides of each husk green; then color both sides of the corn yellow. Next dip a cotton swab into a paint color and dab it onto the blank side of the corn to make kernels. Use a different swab for each paint color and cover the corn with the colorful kernels. When the paint is dry, spread glue on the bottom portion of the painted side of the corn and attach the husks. Once the glue is dry, roll each husk around a pencil to curl its ends. Punch a hole at the top of the corn and tie on a yarn hanger. Finish the ornament by having each student write her name under her poem. Encourage each youngster to give her ornament to a special someone for Thanksgiving!

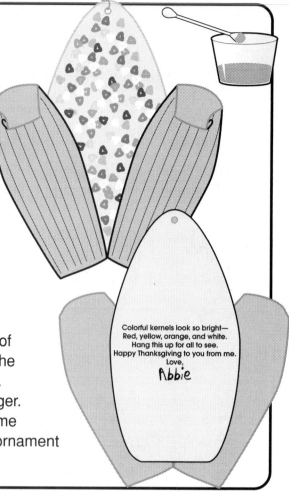

Colorful kernels look so bright—
Red, yellow, orange, and white.
Hang this up for all to see.
Happy Thanksgiving to you from me.
Love,
Abbie

This Little Pilgrim

Feast your students' eyes on these predictable, repetitive language booklets. Give one copy each of pages 51 and 52 to each child. To make a booklet, each child colors the pages, then cuts them apart on the heavy lines. Next, he colors the food pictures and cuts them apart. He matches each picture to the correct page, then glues it in place. On the last page of the book, he draws a self-portrait. When the glue is dry, help him assemble his book and staple it along the left side. This little Pilgrim made a booklet!

THIS LITTLE PILGRIM BY Michael

This little Pilgrim brought a turkey.

This little Pilgrim brought corn.

This little Pilgrim brought sweet potatoes.

This little Pilgrim br

And this little Pilgrim stopped by to say, "I hope you have a happy Thanksgiving Day!"

Name

The First Thanksgiving

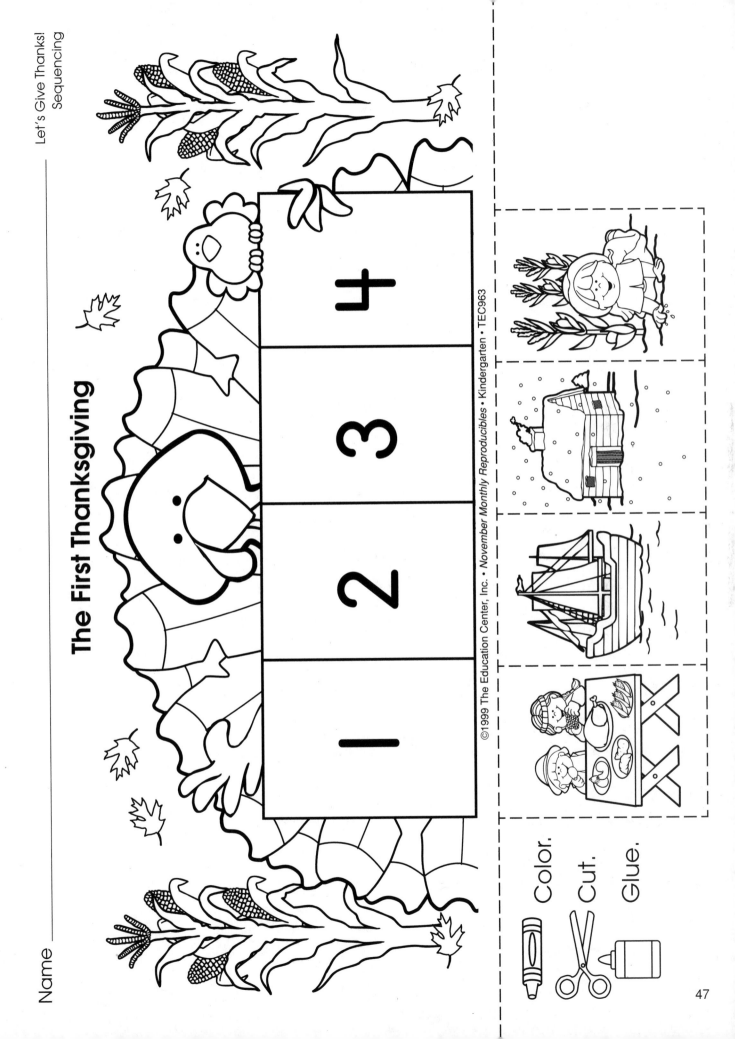

| 1 | 2 | 3 | 4 |

©1999 The Education Center, Inc. • November Monthly Reproducibles • Kindergarten • TEC963

Color.

Cut.

Glue.

Turkey Cards

Use with "Turkey Feather Match" on page 45.

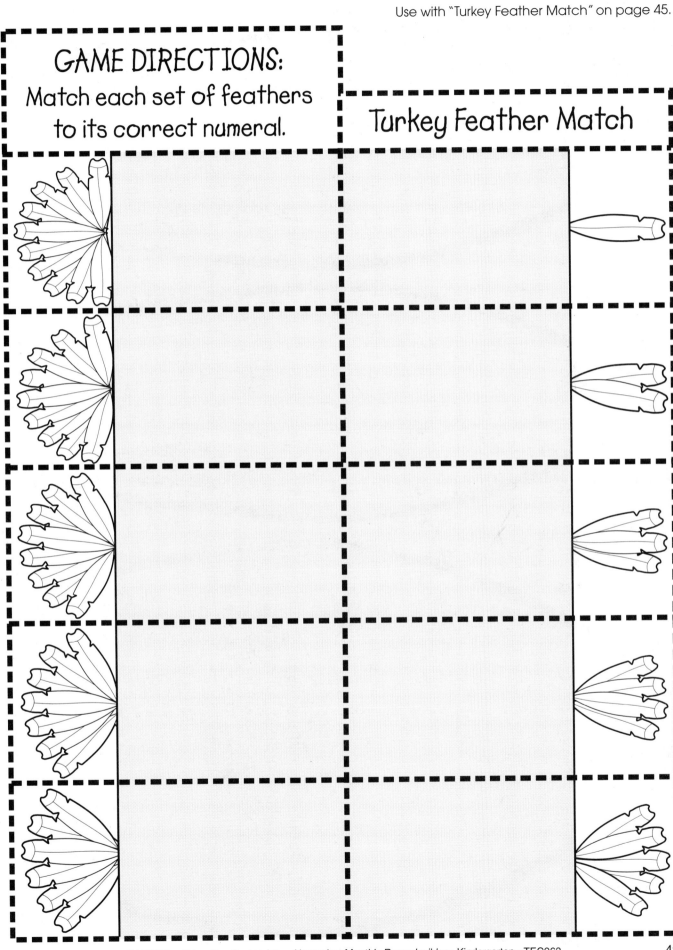

GAME DIRECTIONS:
Match each set of feathers to its correct numeral.

Turkey Feather Match

49

Patterns

Use with "An 'A-maize-ing' Gift" on page 46.

husks

corn

Colorful kernels look so bright—
Red, yellow, orange, and white.
Hang this up for all to see.
Happy Thanksgiving to you from me.
Love,

©1999 The Education Center, Inc.

THIS LITTLE PILGRIM

BY _____

©1999 The Education Center, Inc. • *November Monthly Reproducibles* • Kindergarten • TEC963

1

This little Pilgrim brought a **turkey**.

2

This little Pilgrim brought **corn**.

3

This little Pilgrim brought **sweet** potatoes.

4

This little Pilgrim brought **squash**.

5

And this little Pilgrim stopped by to say,
"I hope you have a happy Thanksgiving Day!"

6

©1999 The Education Center, Inc. • *November Monthly Reproducibles* • Kindergarten • TEC963

National Game And Puzzle Week

Puzzled over activities to do during the last week in November? Observe National Game And Puzzle Week with these fun ideas!

Name Puzzles

Puzzles and names are a perfect fit in this activity. To prepare, gather a class supply of sentence strips and duplicate a large supply of the puzzle pieces on page 54 onto construction paper. Each child will need a number of puzzle pieces equal to the number of letters in her name. This number should include two end pieces. Have a helper assist you in cutting out the puzzle pieces ahead of time. When you are ready to begin, give each child her puzzle pieces and ask her to work with them on a tabletop until she can make a connected line of pieces, with a flat edge at each end of the line. Have her write one letter of her name on each puzzle piece to spell her name. Then give her a sentence strip and have her glue her completed name puzzle on the strip. Fit the strip to the child's head and staple the ends together. It's a puzzle…it's a headband…it's fun!

Let's Play A Game!

The next time your youngsters are game for a game, you'll be prepared with this handy gameboard that you can tailor to fit your curriculum needs. To make the gameboard, duplicate pages 55 and 56 onto sturdy tagboard. Cut out the board along the bold lines; then glue it together as indicated. Laminate the board for multiple uses, such as the ones listed here.

Try the following options for having players move along the board:
— Each player tosses a coin. If it lands on heads, she moves one space; tails, two spaces.
— Each player rolls a die and moves the number of spaces indicated.
— Using programmed cards, have a player draw a card and identify the letter, numeral, shape, or color on the card. If she is correct, she may move one space. Otherwise, play moves to the next player.
— On each player's turn, ask a question related to your current unit of study. If a player answers correctly, she may move one space. Otherwise, play moves to the next player.

If desired, program the spaces on the board with letters, numerals, shapes, or colors. As a player lands on each square, she must identify the symbol or color in order to remain on the square.

For added fun, change the game markers to correspond with the season or your current unit of study. For example, use tiny shells during a beach unit or peppermint discs at Christmas. Here are some other options for playing pieces:

- plastic counters
- shaped miniature erasers
- small, wrapped candies
- thematic stickers on pennies
- buttons
- plastic cubes
- dried pasta

53

Puzzle Pieces

Use with "Name Puzzles" on page 53.

START

FIN

Gameboard

Use with "Let's Play A Game!" on page 53.

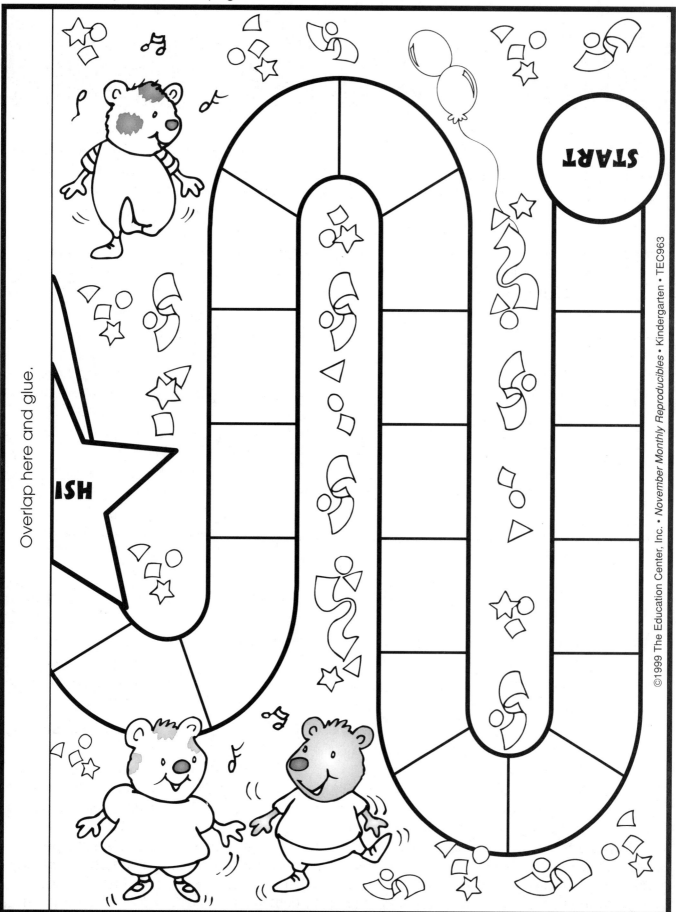

Overlap here and glue.

START

FINISH

Ready For Winter

Whether they head south, head into a cave, or head out into the snow to look for food, winter brings changes in most animals' behavior. Use the ideas in this unit to supplement your teaching about animals preparing for the cold.

Winter Scene Graphing

Literature leads to math with this storytime follow-up activity. Share a good book about animals preparing for winter weather from the list below. Then duplicate a copy of page 59 for each child. Discuss the picture and the various animals shown on the reproducible. Which animals were mentioned in the story you shared? Ask each child to count and graph the animals pictured at the bottom of her sheet.

Time To Sleep
Written & Illustrated by Denise Fleming
Published by Henry Holt And Company, Inc.

Winter
Written by Ron Hirschi
Published by Puffin Books

Dear Rebecca, Winter Is Here
Written by Jean Craighead George
Published by HarperCollins Children's Books

Red Bird Rhyming

Match the words and feed the birds! Give each child a copy of page 60. Go over the names for each of the pictures. Then invite each student to cut out the pictures at the bottom of his sheet and match each one to its rhyming picture on a bird feeder. Have him glue the pictures in place.

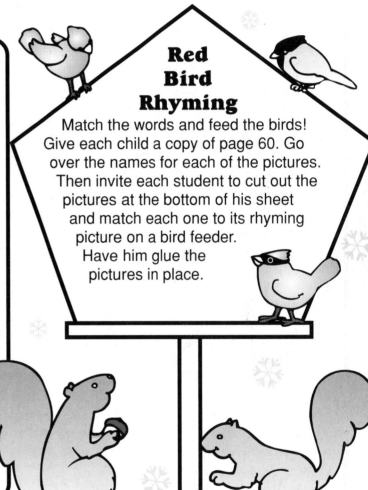

Squirrel, Squirrel, Deer...

Feet are the focus of this patterning activity. To prepare students for a discussion of animal tracks in the snow, first have them examine their own feet—or, actually, their shoes! Invite your group to make a pattern based on the characteristics of their shoes, such as *red shoes, white shoes, red shoes, white shoes.* Or how about *tie, buckle, buckle, tie, buckle, buckle?* Then explain that just as people wear different types of shoes, animals have different types of feet. Give each child a copy of page 61. Have everyone look at the tracks at the bottom of the sheet as you identify each animal. Talk about the different shapes and sizes of animal feet. Then invite youngsters to complete each pattern by cutting out and gluing the correct track in the shaded box.

Oh, Nuts!

Stockpile some beginning-sounds skills with this activity that focuses on the sound of *N*. To prepare, gather a few smooth, unshelled nuts, such as acorns or pecans. On all but one of the nuts, use a permanent black marker to write the letter *N*. Leave the remaining nut unmarked. Put all the nuts in a small can or basket. Gather your students in a circle; then pass the container. As each child receives the container, he pulls out a nut and looks for the letter *N*. If the nut is marked, he says a word that begins with the *N* sound, then returns the nut to the container. If his nut is unmarked, he says, "Oh, nuts!" before returning it.

Follow up with the reproducible on page 62. Give each child a copy of the page and direct students to color only the nuts that show a picture of something that begins with the *N* sound.

Winter Animal Memory Game

Encourage students to warm up their memories with the animal cards on page 63. Duplicate two copies of the page; then color the cards and cut them apart to create matching pairs. Invite a pair or small group of students to play a memory game by laying all the cards facedown on a tabletop. Have each player, in turn, flip over two cards, attempting to find a match. If the two cards match, the player may keep them. If the cards do not match, the child flips them back over and play moves to the next child. Continue until all the matches have been found.

Brrr...Bingo!

Is it getting chilly outside? Hibernate in your classroom and play this fun matching game! To prepare, duplicate onto construction paper a class supply of page 64 and a class supply plus one extra of page 63. Cut apart the animal cards on the extra copy of page 63. These will serve as calling cards. Ask each student to cut out her bingo card and eight animal pictures from her copy of page 63; then have her glue the pictures in any order to her bingo card. Provide game markers, such as pennies or plastic chips.

To play, place all the calling cards in a container. Pull out one card at a time, naming the animal shown or actually showing the card to the players. If a child has that animal on her bingo card, she covers it with a marker. Once a child has covered all eight of her spaces, she calls out, "Brrr...Bingo!" If desired, continue until all players have covered their cards.

Name_____

In The Cold

How many?
Count.
Graph.

	1	2	3	4	5	6

Red Bird Rhyming

Cut.

Glue.

Tracks In The Snow

Complete each pattern.

Cut.

Glue.

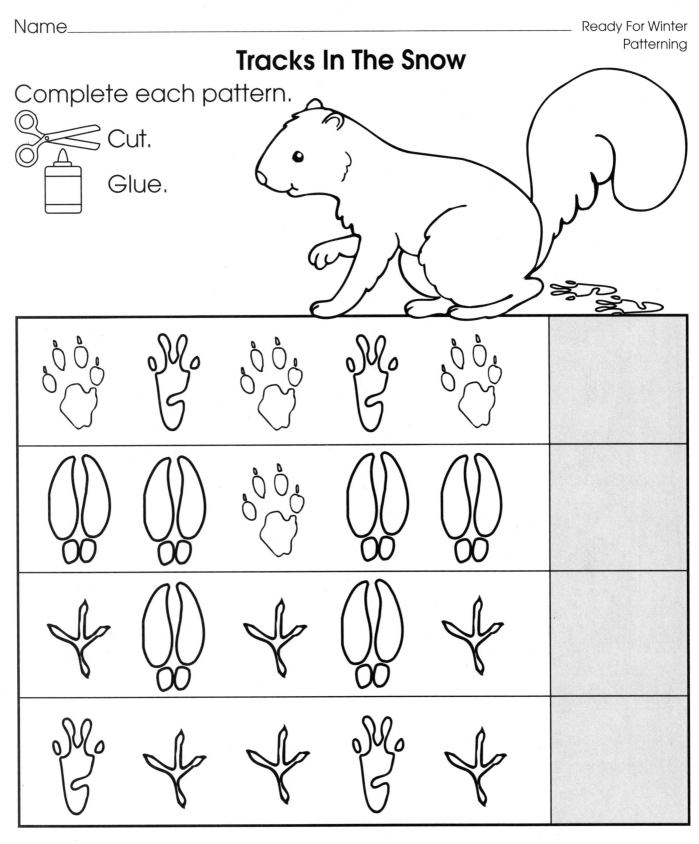

Name_____

Nuts In A Nest

Color the nuts that show things that begin with the sound of *N*.

Bonus Box: Draw something that begins with the *N* sound on the back of this paper.

Bingo Card

Use with "Brrr...Bingo!" on page 58.

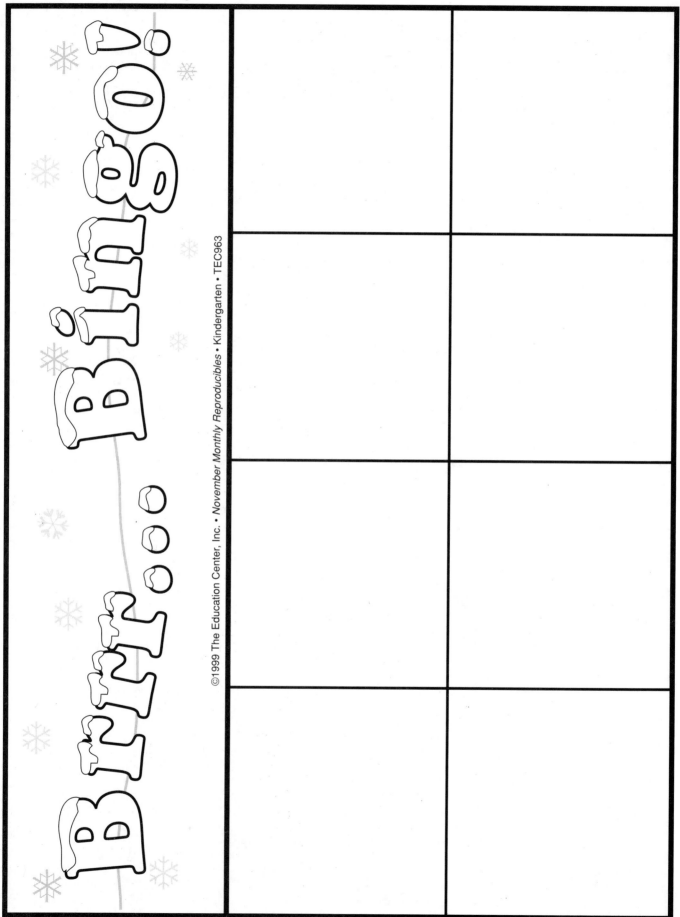